I is for IOWA PEOPLE

I is for IOWA PEOPLE

written by **Mary Ann Gensicke**

illustrated by **Lonna Nachtigal**

IOWA STATE UNIVERSITY PRESS / AMES

Mary Ann Gensicke is a media specialist for the Cedar Rapids Community School District. She received her BA in elementary education from the University of Iowa and her MA in library science from the University of Northern Iowa. A former elementary schoolteacher, she is a member of the Cedar Rapids Area Reading Council and the Iowa Reading Association.

Lonna Nachtigal is a freelance designer and illustrator. She received her BFA from the University of Wisconsin-Eau Claire and worked in Wisconsin public television. She now lives on Onion Creek Farm near Ames, Iowa.

Gensicke and Nachtigal collaborated on a previous book, *I is for Iowa* (1995).

All acknowledgments appear at the end of the book.

© 2001 Iowa State University Press, Ames, Iowa 50014
except for all line art © 2001 Lonna Nachtigal

♾ Printed on acid-free paper in the United States of America

First edition 2001

Library of Congress Cataloging-in-Publication Data

Gensicke, Mary Ann
   I is for Iowa people / written by Mary Ann Gensicke; illustrated by
Lonna Nachtigal.—1st ed.
      p. cm.
Includes bibliographical references.
   ISBN 0-8138-2433-8
   1. Iowa—Biography—Juvenile literature. 2. English language—Alphabet—
Juvenile literature. [1. Iowa—Biography. 2. Alphabet.] I. Nachtigal, Lonna, ill. II. Title.
CT234 .G46 2001
920.0777—dc21   2001001886

Last digit is the print number: 9 8 7 6 5 4 3 2 1

To the Iowa child - our future
Be proud of your heritage!

This book was written in memory of
my father who, as a young engineer in the 1930s,
surveyed many of the fields and farmlands
across the state for the purpose of building roads
that would connect the state of Iowa to the nation.

Meet some of Iowa's interesting people!

A a is for

Astronauts

Some people dream of traveling into outer space. Outer space is the vast area beyond the earth's atmosphere. The atmosphere is the blanket of air in which we all live.

Seven Iowans had their dreams come true when they were chosen

Laurel B. Clark
Mission specialist, Ames

R. Walter Cunningham
Astronaut, Creston

David C. Hilmers
Astronaut, Clinton

James M. Kelly
Pilot, Burlington

2

to train as U.S. astronauts at the Johnson Space Center in Houston, Texas. Although some of these people were not selected for space travel, they have all played important roles in the exploration of outer space.

George D. Nelson
Astronaut, Charles City

Loren J. Shriver
Astronaut, Jefferson

Peggy A. Whitson
Mission specialist, Mt. Ayr

Bb

is for

Mildred Wirt Benson

"HE'S ESCAPED!" NANCY EXCLAIMED AS SHE SURVEYED
THE CONFUSION.

THE BUNGALOW
MYSTERY

Born in Ladora, Iowa, in 1905, Mildred Benson became a journalist, a pilot, and a writer. She has written over 100 books for children and young adults, many of them mysteries. Sometimes she wrote using her own name as author, but more often she used one of several pen names.

Nancy Drew, girl detective, is the heroine of her most famous series. Under the pen name "Carolyn Keene," Mildred wrote the first Nancy Drew book *The Secret of the Old Clock* in 1930. Nancy Drew solved mysteries in 23 books that have entertained generations of young readers.

Cc

is for

Arthur Collins

Radios fascinated young Arthur Collins. In 1918 he made his first two-way radio from a Quaker Oats box, a wire from a Model T Ford, and some telephone parts. He was nine years old, and this was one of the first radios in Iowa. When he was 14, Arthur passed the test to become a radio operator and began talking to people all over the world.

After college, Arthur started a company in Cedar Rapids to make parts for radios. The Collins Radio Company grew to be one of the largest companies in Iowa and a world leader in making airplane radio equipment. Admiral Byrd, on the first flight to the South Pole, used Collins radio transmitters. Astronaut Neil Armstrong, on the first flight to the moon, also used Collins transmitters to talk to the people back home in the United States.

Arthur Collins broadcasts by ham radio from his garden shed.

Dd
is for
Grenville M. Dodge

During the Civil War, General Grenville Dodge fought for the North in the 4th Iowa Infantry. He was skilled at building the bridges and railroad tracks that helped move troops to the front lines of battle. Even President Abraham Lincoln asked his advice on railroads.

Union Pacific train in 1871.

After the war, General Dodge became chief engineer for the Union Pacific Railroad and took charge of completing the first railroad to cross the North American continent. He later worked on rail lines in the southwestern United States and in Cuba. Because of his railroad work, General Dodge became a rich man. He built a mansion in Council Bluffs that is a museum today. Fort Dodge is named for the general.

Ee

is for
Simon Estes

The voice of Simon
Estes has been heard
around the world.
He has sung for
kings, queens, popes,
and presidents.

SIMON ESTES

"Great voice—highest degree
of interpretation."
—Pravda (Moscow)

"He left the audience
shouting in the aisles—wildly
demanding more."
—Sunday Telegraph (Sydney)

"Rolling voluminous sound."
—Time Magazine

"Perfection—a voice
with beauty of velvet, strength
of steel."
—La Stampa (Turin)

He has performed in the world's finest opera houses and recital halls with the best orchestras and conductors.

Simon grew up in Centerville, Iowa, in a poor family with three sisters and one brother. He sang in church and he sang in school. When he got to SUI, now the University of Iowa, he sang in a group called the Old Gold Singers. There, one of his teachers encouraged him to pursue a singing career. Simon did so. He overcame many difficulties to become a very well-known singer. Today he encourages young people to develop and share their talents.

Ff
is for
First Ladies

The woman who is married to the president of the United States is called the first lady. Two first ladies were born in Iowa.

Lou Henry Hoover was born in Waterloo in 1875 and was married to the 31st president, Herbert Hoover. Mrs. Hoover was

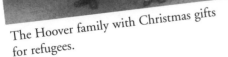

The Hoover family with Christmas gifts for refugees.

highly educated and spoke five languages well. She worked for the Girl Scouts of America, serving as their national president.

Mamie Doud Eisenhower was born in Boone in 1896 and also lived in Cedar Rapids. Her husband, Dwight Eisenhower, was the 34th president. Mrs. Eisenhower was warm and friendly and one of the world's most-admired women.

(above) The Eisenhower family in the White House, Christmas 1957, and (below) Mrs. Eisenhower shares her flowers, Easter 1968.

Gg
is for
Dan Gable

Dan Gable's goal was to become the best wrestler in his weight class. He practiced with a barbell set his father gave him for his 13th birthday. At Waterloo West High School, Dan won every wrestling match, and at Iowa State University he lost only one. Dan says that vision, faith, and a bit of luck helped him win 182 matches in school and college and a gold medal at the 1972 Olympic games.

The gold is given to the best wrestler in the world that year.

After the Olympics, Dan became the head wrestling coach at the University of Iowa. He was a great coach, and his teams won many Big Ten titles and national championships. He also coached 10 other Olympic winners. "I like coaching champions rather than being a champion myself," he said.

Dan was so good at his sport that he was chosen for both the USA Wrestling Hall of Fame and the Olympic Hall of Fame.

Hh is for

Jesse Hiatt

Madison County farmer Jesse Hiatt liked to grow new types of apples, berries, and flowers.

He planted an apple orchard
to raise fruit for his family,
and one of the trees bore
apples that were long and firm
and full of flavor.
Jesse named the apple
"Hawkeye" to honor the state
of Iowa. When he entered it
in a contest, it was chosen as
the best apple in the world. A
nursery in Missouri bought
the right to grow the winning
apple and renamed it
the "Delicious."

Jesse Hiatt and his wife Rebecca.

Ii

is for Ioway Indians

An Ioway man smokes a ceremonial pipe.

The Ioway Indians gave their name to our state. The men and women of this Native American tribe were the first people to live

on the land that is now Iowa. They hunted elk, deer, and buffalo. As the animals moved, the people in the tribe followed them.

In 1838, led by Chief Mahaska (or White Cloud), they sold the rights to all of their lands in the Iowa Territory for $157,500. Then they moved to a reservation where the Nemaha River joins the Missouri River.

Jj

is for Rebecca Johnson

Widow Rebecca Johnson of Maxwell had to find a way to support her three young children. She became a poultry farmer and kept her henhouse so warm that the hens laid eggs all winter long. To hatch the eggs into baby chicks, she built an incubator.

Rebecca Johnson celebrates a large, successful chick brood, 1910.

An incubator keeps many more eggs at the right temperature for hatching than a mother hen can. Mrs. Johnson was then able to hatch 5,000 chicks in one season.

Many people asked her for advice on hatching and raising chicks, so in 1906 she wrote a book to help them, *How to Hatch, Brood, Feed, and Prevent Chicks from Dying in the Shell.* Mrs. Johnson also invented an alarm that sounded when the farmer should adjust the temperature within the incubator.

Kk is for
Nile Kinnick

In grade school, Nile's favorite game was football.

(below) Nile holds the Heisman Trophy, for the best college football player of the year 1939.

Scholar and athlete Nile Kinnick was born in Adel in 1918. He played baseball, basketball, and football at the University of Iowa but was best known for his skill at playing football. When he was in his last year in college, he won top classroom awards as well as the Heisman Trophy for the best college football player in the nation.

Nile entered law school, following in the footsteps of his grandfather, a former Iowa governor. But the world was at war so, after one year, he left school and joined the Navy Air Corps Reserve. In 1943, when he was only 24, the plane Nile was flying disappeared into the Pacific Ocean.

Today the football stadium at the University of Iowa is named in his honor.

L1
is for
Robert Lucas

Robert Lucas was the first governor of the Iowa Territory in 1838. During his time in office, many laws were passed. One of the most important laws started free schools in every town in the territory. These schools were for young people between the ages of four and twenty-one.

Plum Grove, the home of Iowa's first governor and his wife.

In 1844 Governor Lucas moved the capital of Iowa from Burlington to a beautiful site on the Iowa River. The new capital was named Iowa city. There, the governor and his wife, Friendly, built a home they called Plum Grove. Today that home is a national landmark.

Mm

is for
Meskwaki

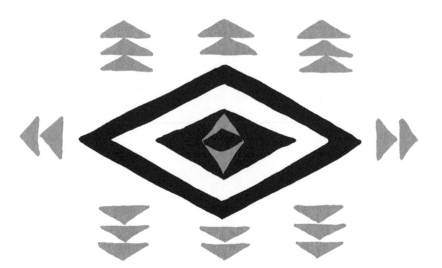

The Meskwaki are Native Americans of the Sac and Fox tribe, who have lived in Iowa since before the settlers came in the 1800s.

Traditional Meskwaki dance at the powwow held during the August full moon. *Photo by Robert Campagna.*

They own over 7,000 acres of land in central Iowa, near the town of Tama. Their land is called a *settlement* and the people own the land together. This means that no family owns any part by itself. A tribal council makes decisions about the settlement. Children go to school on the settlement or in Tama.

Every year the Meskwaki hold a summer powwow. This is a get-together where they dance traditional Indian dances and display their crafts. The Meskwaki are known for beautiful beadwork.

Nn
is for
George P. Nissen

George Nissen of Cedar Rapids invented the trampoline we know today. He liked to jump and tumble, and this was a way to do it better.

George Nissen trampolining with a kangaroo.

At the University of Iowa, George won the national championships in tumbling and in diving. After college, he started Nissen Trampoline Company to make sports equipment. George's kind of trampolining became an Olympic sport in the year 2000.

George has traveled the world, performing and telling people about trampolining. Once he jumped with a kangaroo. That caught people's attention. Besides the trampoline, George invented more than 40 pieces of sports equipment. "Love, work, and creating," he says, "are the three things that make people happiest."

O o is for
Old Order Amish

Buggies drive past an Old Order Amish farm near Kalona.

Members of the Old Order Amish society wear very simple, dark clothes. Sometimes they are called the "plain people" because of the way they live and dress. They travel by horse and buggy. The buggy is always black.

These quiet Iowans live on family farms. They raise corn, barley, oats, and hay and use horses for fieldwork. Old Order Amish families often have eight to ten children. The boys help with farm work, like pulling weeds and feeding hogs. The girls help with the housework.

The Amish share common beliefs. They believe in peace and not in war. For them, Sunday is the most important day of the week. They teach their children in their own way in Amish schools. The Old Order always help other Amish families in trouble.

Amish children at school.
Photos by John M. Zielinski.

P p
is for
Austin Palmer

Penmanship and Palmer go hand in hand. Austin Palmer worked in Cedar Rapids with an insurance company.

Before typewriters or computers, companies needed clear handwriting for their records. So Palmer thought of another way of writing. People could use the way they sat, their arm movements, and their finger positions to make nice, round, free-flowing letters.

To spread his handwriting method, Palmer taught classes. He opened a business college and started a magazine. He also traveled around the country showing teachers the new way to write. Teachers in New York state were the first to use the Palmer method of writing. By 1920 the method had spread to schools across America and around the world.

Qq
is for Quakers

Quakers are a religious group whose members are called *Friends.* They hold simple church services in meetinghouses where there is no minister and anyone may speak. Quaker settlers came to Iowa in the 1830s. They built the towns of West Branch and New Providence. Two of the schools they started are open today, the Scattergood School and William Penn University.

The Quakers hated slavery. In the nineteenth century they helped to run Iowa's Underground Railroad. It was a secret escape route. Runaway slaves were smuggled from house to house along the "railroad" until they reached safety. In the twentieth century, Iowa Friends sheltered German Jews out of Hitler's reach.

The Quakers were the first religious group in the United States to give equal rights to women. President Herbert Hoover came from a Quaker family in West Branch.

German refugees outside Hickory Grove meetinghouse, Scattergood, 1939.

Rr is for
Donna Reed

Donnabelle Mullenger left school in Denison at age 16 and caught a train to Los Angeles. There she joined an acting school, won a beauty contest, shortened her name, and was offered a part in a movie. Donna went on to act in over 40 films. People still watch *It's a Wonderful Life*. She also starred in her own TV series, the *Donna Reed Show.*

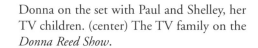

Donna on the set with Paul and Shelley, her TV children. (center) The TV family on the *Donna Reed Show*.

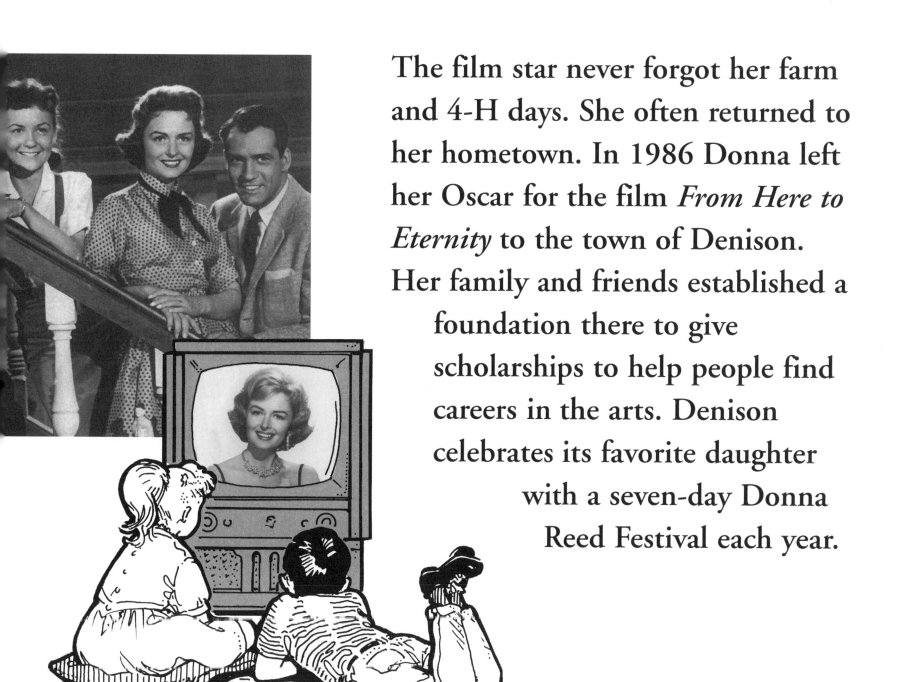

The film star never forgot her farm and 4-H days. She often returned to her hometown. In 1986 Donna left her Oscar for the film *From Here to Eternity* to the town of Denison. Her family and friends established a foundation there to give scholarships to help people find careers in the arts. Denison celebrates its favorite daughter with a seven-day Donna Reed Festival each year.

Ss is for Kate Shelley

Fifteen-year-old Kate Shelley risked her life to save others. One July night in 1881, a terrible storm washed out the railroad bridge over Honey Creek near the Shelley's home outside Boone. Kate heard the sound of an engine falling into the water and the cries of the men who were trapped. The midnight train would be coming from the west, full of passengers, and the bridge was out. There were no telephones. To get help, Kate crawled on her hands and knees in the rain across the high Des Moines River trestle bridge. Then she ran to the Moingona Station and warned the station agent to stop the Northwestern express and rescue the engineers in Honey Creek.

The story of Kate's bravery was sent all over Iowa and across the nation. She was called "the Iowa heroine." The Iowa General Assembly gave her a gold medal. The present railroad bridge, built in 1901, is named for Kate.

(far left) The trestle railroad bridge over the Des Moines River.
(left) Kate Shelley at the railroad station that she made famous as a girl.

T t

is for
John Tokheim

Tokheim

When he was 16 years old, John left his home in the country of Norway and set out for faraway Iowa. He worked on a farm,

A car fills up at Tokheim's "Triune" pump.

then he opened a hardware store. At that time, hardware stores sold kerosene fuel for lamps and stoves. John disliked the smell of kerosene on his hands, so he did something about it. He invented a pump that sent the kerosene up from an underground storage tank and into a bucket without hands having to touch it. This was the beginning of the gasoline pump we know today.

To make the pumps, John started the Tokheim Manufacturing Company in Cedar Rapids. He made many other inventions in his lifetime.

Uu

is for Dyer Usher

A bag of salt and a gun were all that 16-year-old Dyer Usher had when he first came to Iowa. He swam across the Mississippi River to visit an Indian village near Dubuque. From there he walked to Omaha and back again to see what the land was like.

Before bridges were built, the way to cross a river was to take a ferryboat. Dyer became a ferryman on the Mississippi near Muscatine. He carried people and goods from one side to the other in his boat.

In 1838 Iowa was opened to settlers. Dyer's large family all came to claim land along the Red Cedar River, near what is now Cedar Rapids. Dyer took people across the Cedar River in a flatboat that he pushed with a pole. A small town grew up at his crossing place called Ushers Ferry. Today children visit Ushers Ferry Historic Village to learn about life in early Iowa.

V

is for
James Van Allen

Sending satellites into space is one of the interesting things James Van Allen has done. Dr. Van Allen is an expert in the study of outer space. Working as a professor of physics at the University of Iowa, he discovered new facts about the layers of air surrounding the earth.

Dr. Van Allen found that the earth is circled by two bands, or belts, of high-energy particles. These belts can be harmful to satellites and astronauts. The bands are named the "Van Allen Radiation Belts" in his honor. Knowing about them helps us understand the universe in which we live.

Dr. Van Allen at the North Liberty Radio Observatory.

Van Allen's discovery in 1958 helped scientists design the rockets and space shuttles that put people into space a few years later.

Ww

is for the Willsons

When people hear "76 Trombones" they think of Mason City. It is a song from Meredith Willson's famous Broadway musical, *The Music Man*. In it, Willson calls Mason City, his hometown,

Meredith Willson leads the band in Mason City. (bottom) Dixie Willson in Hollywood, 1936.

"River City." A man who arrives to sell musical instruments first has to teach all the children in River City to play in a band.

The Willson family loved playing music, acting, and writing. Meredith played the flute and piccolo in Mason City. When he grew up, he studied music in New York and became a performer and a conductor as well as a composer.

Meredith's sister, Dixie, was an elephant rider in the Ringling Brothers' Circus for a while. Later, she became a well-known writer of poetry, short stories, and children's books. Four of her stories were made into movies.

X x

is for Explorers

Captain Meriwether Lewis and Lieutenant William Clark were two explorers (*X* is a really hard one!) of the land of Iowa. They were sent by President Jefferson to report on the new territory west of the Mississippi River. The nation had just bought that land from France for 15 million dollars (about 3 cents an acre).

The Lewis and Clark expedition set out to find the source of the Missouri

River and to look for the best places to build trading posts and forts. They started from St. Louis with three boats. Poling a keelboat upriver, it took 60 days to reach Iowa. As they traveled along what is now the western border of the state, Lewis and Clark met the Missouri and Otoe Indians. They wrote down everything they saw in their journals and sent letters to President Jefferson telling what the country was like.

The only man to lose his life on the expedition was Sergeant Charles Floyd. He died of fever along the Floyd River, which was named after him. The town of Sergeant Bluff and a monument in Sioux City also remember this first explorer to be buried in Iowa soil.

Captain Meriwether
Lewis, 1807

Lieutenant William
Clark, 1810

Yy
is for George Henry Yewell

At the age of 11, George Yewell moved with his mother from the East Coast to Iowa City.

Yewell with his portrait of Governor Samuel Kirkwood.

He began work as a tailor, learning how to make and repair clothing. But George liked to draw. A cartoon he drew about moving the capital from Iowa City to Fort Des Moines went all over the state. People asked for more. Soon George became a well-known artist. At that time, Iowa was a new state. His pencil sketches and drawings were some of the first of the Iowa City area. He also painted pictures of famous Iowans, including several early governors of the state.

Zz

is for

Jo Ann Zimmerman

In 1987 Jo Ann Zimmerman was the first woman to be elected lieutenant governor of the State of Iowa. Ms. Zimmerman is a nurse who wanted to make laws about healthcare. In the Iowa government, she worked on a law to put health education classes in all Iowa schools. When she became president of the Iowa senate, Zimmerman supported a law to stop smoking in the workplace. She also helped pass more health and education laws. One law gives money to talented and gifted school programs. Another gives money to libraries so they can share materials.

Ms. Zimmerman grew up on a farm in Van Buren County. Today she and her husband are cattle farmers.

Donna Reed reads to Patti Petersen,
her TV daughter.

Children are made readers on the laps of their parents.

–Emilie Buchwa

What better way to share Iowa history with young people than through the pages of a book? The written word is the bond between generations. In this book, my purpose is to reflect on the lives of Iowans, past and present, and to record those things that have a permanent value or a curious human interest. I have included groups as well as single people. For certain letters of the alphabet, groups stretched my ability to include important Iowans within the confines of the 26-letter framework.

As I began reading about the men and women who are the "stars" in the history of the state, I became aware that these people were and are remarkable. They used their gifts and talents to make the world around them a better or more interesting place to live. These were people who dreamed and worked, even failed at times, and yet they succeeded. The more I read, the more the project became a labor of love. There were times when I found myself peering beyond the words I could use on the pages of this book to take a close look at the human being about whom I was writing.

The longer I worked on the text, the more I felt a duty to tell the children of our state about the people whose lives I was studying. The difficulty came in deciding who to place in and who to leave out. Countless outstanding Iowans could have been featured. If the alphabet framework was confining, an even greater challenge was trying to sculpt the significance of a person's lifetime into just a paragraph or two of text.

There are many omissions in this book. In general, the text is designed to reach younger readers, so the pages are not laden with dates and names. I have left out facts and people that other writers might deem significant. This does not lessen the importance of the people who were omitted; it simply says that they would be more appropriately discussed in a book with a different purpose. Those who desire to read further will find ample information in other books and references.

Throughout the book, there is an attempt to make the past serve the present and motivate young people of today to look into the future. Children belong to the future; and we need to prepare them for it. Education is a doorway and a gate. In the doorway, young people stand at the threshold of other worlds. It is through the gate that they enter the future carved out for them. Each generation must serve its own ends and live its own life. It must make its own mistakes and learn its own lessons. However, it would be hopeless if each generation could not learn from the generation that preceded it.

It is with a great deal of humbleness that I address the lives of historically notable Iowa men and women. Our state was not made great, rich, or proud in a day. The lines of those laboring in the fields are long. Each person who stood in those lines did something and left something behind for future generations. It is my belief that what these people have accomplished is worth recording, even in short form, for the youngest readers in our schools.

To those of you who thumb through these pages – may this book further your appreciation of the uniqueness of our state and raise your pride in the accomplishments of its people.

I am greatly indebted to a number of people for assistance and encouragement. A huge thank-you goes to my family, whose patience has been never ending while I discussed book entries and discoveries with them more times than they would have chosen!

I am also grateful to the present day "stars" of our state, who graciously opened their photo files and thoughts and assisted me in representing them correctly.

I appreciate the writers and researchers who preceded me in recording facts about significant Iowans. Their work greatly shortened the time it took to generate ideas for this book. I have spent many hours reading historical documents about the state and its people, only to be reminded that human endeavor is a cumulative effort. I traveled a well-beaten track that others trod before me. The difference in this book is that it is written for younger readers.

Many thanks to the staff at the State Historical Society of Iowa in Iowa City, for helping to locate photos and discussing possible entries.

My gratitude also goes to Art Fischbeck, Terry Harrison, and Katrina Bowen of Mason City for their insight into the lives of Meredith and Dixie Willson. Sandy Bailen Scott of Denison was very helpful in securing photos of Donna Reed and acquiring permissions for their use.

I also thank the staff at Iowa State University Press for realizing that Iowans are always eager to read more about their past, their present, and their future.

A final thank-you, perhaps the most significant one, goes to all the librarians, teachers, parents, and children around the state of Iowa who expressed interest in my first book, *I is for Iowa*. They were the inspiration to share more of who we are and what we are all about as a state. May those whose lives I have touched know that they, in spirit if not in words, are included between the covers of this book as people who have helped to make Iowa the great state that it is.

Grateful acknowledgment to the following for permission to publish their photographs:

A: NASA (National Aeronautics and Space Administration), Houston, Texas
B: Mildred Wirt Benson, Toledo, Ohio
C: Collins Radio Company, Cedar Rapids, Iowa
D: State Historical Society of Iowa - Des Moines
E: Simon Estes International Foundation for Children, Zurich, Switzerland
F: Mamie Eisenhower: Dwight D. Eisenhower Library, Abilene, Kansas. Lou Henry Hoover: Herbert Hoover Presidential Library, West Branch, Iowa
G: University of Iowa Photographic Service, Iowa City
H: State Historical Society of Iowa - Des Moines
I: State Historical Society of Iowa - Des Moines
J: State Historical Society of Iowa - Des Moines
K: Nile Kinnick papers, Special Collections, University of Iowa, Iowa City
L: State Historical Society of Iowa - Des Moines
M: Robert Campagna, Mount Vernon, Iowa
N: George P. Nissen, San Diego, California
O: John M. Zielinski, Kalona, Iowa
P: Masonic Library, Cedar Rapids, Iowa
Q: Michael Aliza, American Friends Service Committee
R: Donna Reed Center for the Performing Arts, Denison, Iowa
S: Boone County Historical Society, Boone, Iowa
T: Dorothy Johnson, Cedar Rapids, Iowa
U: Ushers Ferry Historic Village, Cedar Rapids, Iowa
V: Dr. James A. Van Allen, Iowa City
W: Lee P. Loomis Archive of Mason City History, Mason City Public Library, Iowa
X: Paintings by Charles Willson Peale, courtesy of Independence National Historical Park, Philadelphia
Y: State Historical Society of Iowa - Des Moines
Z: Jo Ann Zimmerman, West Des Moines
Afterword: Donna Reed Center for the Performing Arts, Denison, Iowa, and the children of Donna Reed

Bibliography

Ambrose, Stephen E., and Sam Abell (photographer). *Lewis and Clark: Voyage of Discovery.* Washington, D.C., National Geographic Society, 1998.

Baender, Paul, ed. *A Hero Perished: The Diary & Selected Letters of Nile Kinnick.* Iowa City: University of Iowa Press, 1991.

Brewer and Wicke. *The History of Linn County, 1878.* Chicago: Western Historical Company.

Briggs, Ely, ed. *The Palimpsest.* Iowa City: State Historical Society of Iowa, 1938.

Brown, Don Doyle. *Iowa, the Land Across the River.* Des Moines: Wallace-Homestead, 1963.

Brown, Don Doyle. *Tell a Tale of Iowa.* Des Moines: Wallace-Homestead, 1965.

Christensen, Thomas Peter. *The Iowa Indians: A Brief History.* Cedar Rapids: Laurence Press, 1954.

Donna Reed Center for the Performing Arts, http://www.donnareed.org

Hake, Herb. *Iowa Inside Out.* Ames: Iowa State University Press, 1968.

Hastie, Eugene. *High Points of Iowa History.* Perry, Iowa, 1966.

"Iowa Inventors and Inventions from A to Z." *The Goldfinch* (Fall 1998): 4-14.

Johnson Space Center, http://www.jsc.nasa.gov

Kummer, Patricia K. *Iowa.* Mankato: Capstone Press, 1999.

Meyers, Virginia A. "The Brief Iowa Career of George Yewell." *IOWAN* (Fall 1984): 32-37.

Midwest Research Institute, ed. *The Iowa Quick Fact Book.* Topeka: Capper Press, 1991.

Moeller, Hubert L. *Hawkeye Tales.* Palmer, Iowa: Hubert L. Moeller, 1963.

Reida, Bernice and Ann Irwin. *Hawkeye Adventure.* Lake Mills: Graphic Publishing, 1966.

Reida, Bernice and Ann Irwin. *Hawkeye Lore.* Pella: Pella Publishing, 1976.

Schmidt, Duane. *Iowa Pride.* Ames: Iowa State University Press, 1996.

Schwieder, Dorothy, Thomas Morain, and Lynn Nielsen. *Iowa Past to Present: The People and the Prairie.* 2d. ed. Ames: Iowa State University Press, 1991.